Spirit into Sound

The Magic of Music

Mickey Hart

Fredric Lieberman

GRATEFUL DEAD® BOOKS

SPIRIT INTO SOUND: THE MAGIC OF MUSIC

FIRST EDITION
Second Printing

Published by Grateful Dead Books, an imprint of Grateful Dead Productions

Inquiries should be addressed to:
Grateful Dead Books
P.O. Box X
Novato, California 94948
www.dead.net

Printed in Hong Kong through Acid Test Productions

Design: Michael Quinn
Cover Illustration: Chris Pinkerton,
Mackerel Graphics, Tiverton, Rhode Island

ISBN# 1-888358-23-8

Library of Congress# 99-095419

Distributed by Publishers Group West, telephone: 800.788.3123

Visit Mickey on the web at www.mhart.com
email at sis@nbn.com

The publishers will arrange to plant two trees for every tree needed to manufacture the paper for this book.

Contents

Dedication

To all who came before, who have led us to this work, both musicians and teachers. Some gave us skills with which to enter music's magic realms; others inspired our spirit of exploration and the quest for answers to the big questions.
—Mickey and Fred

♪

To my mother Leah, my first teacher; Charles Perry, who refined my technique; and Arthur Jones, band teacher at Lawrence High School, who first opened the door to music's spirit world.

To Tito Puente, Gene Krupa, Buddy Rich, Giovanni Hidalgo Babatunde Olatunji, Hamza El-Din, Alla Rakha, Zakir Hussain, and Airto Moreira.

To Joseph Campbell, Huston Smith, Stanley Krippner, and John Blacking.

To Jerry Garcia, Robert Hunter, Bob Weir, Phil Lesh, Ron Pigpen McKernan, and Bill Kreutzmann: my dear friends and fellow explorers of the Zone.
—Mickey

♪

To Charles Warren Fox, Louis Mennini, Thomas Canning, and Bernard Rodgers, who first nurtured my skills and love of composition.

To John Cage, Lou Harrison, Yoko Ono, and Toru Takemitsu, who brought me into the world of experimental composition and performance.

To Charles Seeger, Mantle Hood, Barbara B. Smith, and Klaus Wachsmann, whose love of learning was infectious, and whose dedication to scholarship inspiring.
—Fred

Introduction

Throughout the ages, people from all cultures have struggled to understand and express the power and beauty of music and explain the magical quality of sound. Although a sheet of music is visible, as is the instrument on which it is played, music itself is invisible, mysterious. There is no satisfactory definition of it; every culture draws the borderlines of sonic events in different places. But everyone agrees that music affects us, moves us, inspires us, and transforms us as human beings. This book is a testament to the power of such sound.

Years ago, when Fred Lieberman and I were researching what were to become *Drumming at the Edge of Magic* and *Planet Drum*, we began stumbling on brilliant quotes, epiphanies that happen in an instant, lighting our world with clarity and wit. We gathered and stored these quotes in our information snake, what we called our **Anaconda**–our ongoing research project in search of the Grail–the explanation for the connection between music and trance.

These wonderful images were full of light and wisdom, somehow speaking the unspeakable, touching the untouchable. In this collection, which is laced with some thoughts and recollections of our own, we try to present the wonder of music in the words of those touched by its magic. Music is a miracle, transforming consciousness, taking the mind and spirit to places unknown.

Using the energy of music to shape that invisible place we call the soul seems appropriate somehow. This dance occurs in a place outside our everyday consciousness, yet it has access to it as well. Good and evil, love and hate, war and peace are all fair game in this domain. All the emotions are courted, and nothing is too weird for the muse. When I think of "spirit into sound," I realize this is what music is all about. How do we turn spirit, which is a feeling, into a reality and energy that we can harness and use? Transmutation. Take ideas and the feelings that we have, and turn them into sound. This is the great work, this is the philosopher's stone, this is the alchemy of life. Music is the gold of the sound-shaper.

The Anaconda has once more shed its skin, revealing gleaming treasures that give new meaning to the world around us: these we dedicate to musicians and music lovers everywhere.

This book is not a museum of old ideas, but rather a living, interactive guide to the future. The power of music is still young, its energy only partly realized. We're continuing to learn to use this gift, to penetrate its mystery, and ultimately to share this knowledge with everyone.

—Mickey Hart

Preface

Fredric Lieberman

One of the most powerful insights afforded by research in ethnomusicology, most clearly articulated by John Blacking, is that music is inseparable from our humanity. Music fills needs at the center of our being, needs not met by other arts or activities, sacred or secular. No human society, present or past, has lacked music. Music is therefore one of the very few human universals, which puts it on the same level as food and sex.

It follows that any tendency to consider music a "luxury" is dangerous. This patently false idea leads to devaluing music in general education, often to the point of eliminating it entirely when budgets are tight. That Plato, Confucius, and many other great thinkers have held music to be the indispensable cornerstone of education should help strengthen the resolve of parents and educators to make music part of every home and to maintain and strengthen music programs in our schools.

From early childhood, my parents encouraged my love of music, which was more likely to express itself through rambling improvisations on the Mason and Hamlin grand piano in our living room than through disciplined practice. I was expected, however, to follow my other love, amateur radio, to a career in electronics engineering. It was something of a surprise—even to me—when I decided to study composition at the Eastman School of Music. And it was also unexpected when, after four years of difficult, competitive, rewarding study at Eastman, I chose to follow an academic career in ethnomusicology.

One of my senior mentors, Dr. Mantle Hood, encouraged his students always to look beyond the ivory tower and write not only for a few dozen specialists, but also for the general reader. I am immensely grateful to Mickey Hart for giving me the opportunity to work with him on a series of books and related projects that have allowed me to follow Dr. Hood's mandate. The partnership with Mickey, which began in 1983 when I first moved to the University of California at Santa Cruz, has been extraordinary. We bring to the table differences in background, personality, and history. When we have not agreed on some point, we have taken these springboards for debate as opportunities rather than problems. The results often surprise both of us. In the present book, I hope our efforts here surprise, entertain, and inspire the reader as well.

Acknowledgments

We wish to thank Caryl Hart and Stacy Kreutzmann Quinn for their inspired arranging and editing which gave this book its rhythm. Thanks to Tom Grady whose vision and skill were a guiding force; Elizabeth Cohen, who asked the right questions, and who brought the Anaconda into the digital domain; John Meyer, whose quest for the perfect loudspeaker made listening a joy, and made Grateful Dead's performances into memorable sonic experiences, building our cathedral of sound; Howard Cohen; Nancy Reid; Michael Quinn; Sherry Sterling; Atesh Sonneborn; Yara Sellin; my daughter, Reya and son, Taro, for their constant support and inspiration.

We invite interested readers to send along their own favorite quotations about music for possible use in future editions of this book. Please e-mail the complete quotation, plus a full citation of its source, to sis@nbn.com.

Music gives a soul to the universe,
wings to the mind,
flight to the imagination,
a charm to sadness,
gaiety and life to everything.
It is the essence of order,
and leads to all that is good,
just and beautiful,
of which it is the invisible,
but never less,
dazzling, passionate, and eternal form.

—Plato

Chapter One

Music and Musicians

Movers and Shakers

The first time I thought of myself as a musician was when I bought a pair of mother-of-pearl bongos at a pawnshop. With these, I gave my first public performance at Atlantic Beach in Long Island. I was about thirteen.

The older kids were building fires and having a party. I sat down, crossed my legs, put the bongos in the sand, and started playing a rhythm, improvising freely as the mood demanded. People gathered around, clapped their hands, and started singing and dancing. It was an instant party, with lots of good-looking girls. For a shy, introverted, skinny kid, this was a major event. I had become Charles Atlas and Errol Flynn, all rolled into one, a fantasy world come true.

I knew right then that I wanted to do this for the rest of my life. It was the call of the wild. It was sexy, it was fun, and it had nothing to do with my parents. Even though I'd been studying military drumming with my mom (a world champion drummer), this was a new world, seductive and irresistible. It was making music in the moment, in the now, feeling not thinking, and provided a foretaste of how I would spend much of my musical life.

Many people have dedicated their lives totally to their own musical quest, often enduring shame, ridicule, and financial hardship to maintain self-respect. Why are they so passionate about an invisible vibration? It must stir the soul—maybe it's even a gift from the gods. But it's not free. Someone had to learn the craft, someone passed it on.

To the outside world some of us are merely recognizable figures within the frenzied celebrity culture of our time. If you are not careful, being a rock star in today's world can kill you. Most everyone lucky enough to fall into this crazy trip knows that by now. That is the dark side you have to dance with. But being a rock star also means that you have lucked out as an artist in this materialistic time and place. It means you can live out the full life of your imagination, if you so wish, and if you survive.

Connecting is the key. The ability to find happiness in your performance, your experience, however brief, on that stage. You practice endless hours, in and out of the dream state, for those few fleeting moments. How you feel after the performance is what you really take home with you.

This is a risky business. It seems as though what you imagine cannot really be accomplished fully on this earth. Only sometimes, in a moment, does it all come together. It is in a blinding flash of the light and sound, a cacophony, that a profusion of images colliding into this marvelous creation becomes your life's work. So rare, so rare—it is no wonder that we are all crazy for this moment. It is like the perfect crime or a miracle, everything coming together in an instant: the marvelous, the miraculous, the magic finally at hand. Who could expect this on a daily basis except the most mad, the artist, the musician.

When performed correctly, music is a never-ending circle of power. The energy achieved in the musical experience is transmuted and passed on in everyday life. Where it can lead you has no limit, no border, as these witnesses so clearly report.

We are the music makers,
And we are the dreamers of dreams,
Wandering by lone sea-breakers,
and setting by desolate streams;
World-losers and world forsakers,
On whom the pale moon gleams:
Yet we are the movers and shakers
Of the world forever, it seems.

—Arthur O'Shaughnessy

Assassins!

–Arturo Toscanini
(to his orchestra after an
unsatisfactory performance)

I have to create.
I have to dig in the earth;
I have to make something grow;
I have to bake something;
I have to write something;
I have to sing something;
I have to put something out.
It's not a need to prove anything.
It's just my way of life.

—Bette Midler

Rock 'n' roll is like a drug. I don't take very much rock 'n' roll, but when I do rock 'n' roll, I fuckin' do it. But I don't want to do it all the time 'cause it'll kill me. When you're singing and playing rock 'n' roll, you're on the leading edge of yourself. You're tryin' to vibrate, tryin' to make something happen. It's like there's somethin' alive and exposed.

—Neil Young

I don't choose what I compose.
It chooses me.

—Gustav Mahler

A wise friend of my father's had said to me: "You should not go into music unless it is a compulsion. In the end, all you really have as a center is the music itself. Make sure that you have to be with it every day. If that's true, then you should become a musician."

—Michael Tilson Thomas

Musical ideas pursue me
to the point of torture.
I cannot get rid of them,
they stand before me like a wall.
If it is an allegro that pursues me,
my pulse beats faster, I cannot sleep;
if an adagio, I find my pulse beating slowly.
My imagination plays upon me as if I were
a keyboard.

—Joseph Haydn

The best way to kill your music is to sit down every day and work at it. You got to sneak up on it and catch it when it's not looking.

—Iggy Pop

There's only two ways to sum up music:
either it's good or it's bad.
If it's good you don't mess about it;
you just enjoy it.

—Louis Armstrong

What's swinging in words?
If a guy makes you tap your foot
and if you feel it down your back,
you don't have to ask anybody
if that's good music or not.
You can always feel it.

—Miles Davis

Many have described the essence of music as representing internal emotional states that cannot be put into words. Every musician knows this. The big question, the big mystery, is how to achieve this transfer of energy, how to translate your feelings into sounding movements and actions, and how these forms communicate so powerfully and precisely the original feelings. This process is, at least in part, what we mean by "Spirit into Sound."

Music is your own experience,
your thoughts,
your wisdom.
If you don't live it,
it won't come out of your horn.
They teach you there is a boundary line to music. But, man, there's no boundary line to art.

—Charlie Parker

I believe my music is the healin' music. I believe my music can make the blind see, the lame walk, the deaf and dumb hear and talk because it inspires and uplifts people. It regenerates the ears, makes the liver quiver, the bladder splatter, and the knees freeze. I'm not conceited, either.

—Little Richard

The drive to create, perform, and reproduce music is common to all mankind, a drive so basic that when a man cannot find an instrument to suit him, he creates his own.

—Joseph Howard

Once I had a dream to live and love,
and this dream became music.
It touched all of the beautiful experiences I
have searched for or known.
Each sound was a color,
and each color was a warm feeling,
and my heart kept the tempo.

—Les McCann

Music is more than a combination of sounds. It is colors too. I see the different keys like a rainbow. The key of D is daffodil yellow, B Major is maroon, and B Flat is blue.

—Marian McPartland

I did not choose my profession, it chose me.
Since childhood, it has grown
between me and people.
My music is all one love letter,
but to whom?

—Ned Rorem

God tells me how the music should sound,
but you stand in the way!

—Arturo Toscanini
(speaking to his orchestra)

Music lasts by itself and cares not who
composed it; nor can music recall
the thousand anonymous fingers and mouths
which tamper with it,
beautifully or badly.

—Ned Rorem

Without a good listener, even the best performer is useless. And if a performer is not a good listener, the performance is useless. The performer must listen to the quiet voice beneath the surface to connect to the music. The performer must also listen to the hall, the audience, the instrument, and the other performers.

All my concerts had no sounds in them:
they were completely silent ...
People had to make their own music in their minds.

—Yoko Ono

If you're not listening to the
person next to you,
then you're just beating stuff up.

—Airto Moreira

It isn't evil that's ruining the earth,
but mediocrity.
The crime is not that Nero played
while Rome burned,
but that he played badly.

—Ned Rorem

My own friends
are those who give good performances.
My enemies
are those who in any way debase music.

—George Bernard Shaw

He who makes a mistake is still our friend;
He who adds to, or shortens,
a melody is still our friend;
But he who violates a rhythm unawares
Can never be our friend.

—Ishaq Ibn Ibrahim

When you play from your heart,
all of a sudden there's no gravity.
You don't feel the weight of the world,
of bills, of anything.
That's why people love it.
Your so-called insurmountable problems disappear,
and instead of problems you get possibilities.

—Carlos Santana

Everything you do is music
and everywhere is the best seat.

—John Cage

Since a Grateful Dead experience depended on high volume levels, and the venues in which we played continually got larger, silences became more important, more noticeable, and more dramatic. To reach this volume required a new technology of amplification that extended the state of the art beyond the typical PA system, which was designed for speech and the delivery of messages, to something that could vibrate all the senses. To deliver this auditory payload, a new science was developed. The lows were lower, the highs higher, the signals cleaner, the silences quieter. A new love affair with sound had begun.

We're working with dynamics now. We've spent two years with loud, and we've spent six months with deafening! I think we're moving out of our loud stage. We've learned, after these last two years, that what's really important is that the music be groovy, and if it's groovy enough and it's well-played enough, it doesn't have to be loud.

—Jerry Garcia

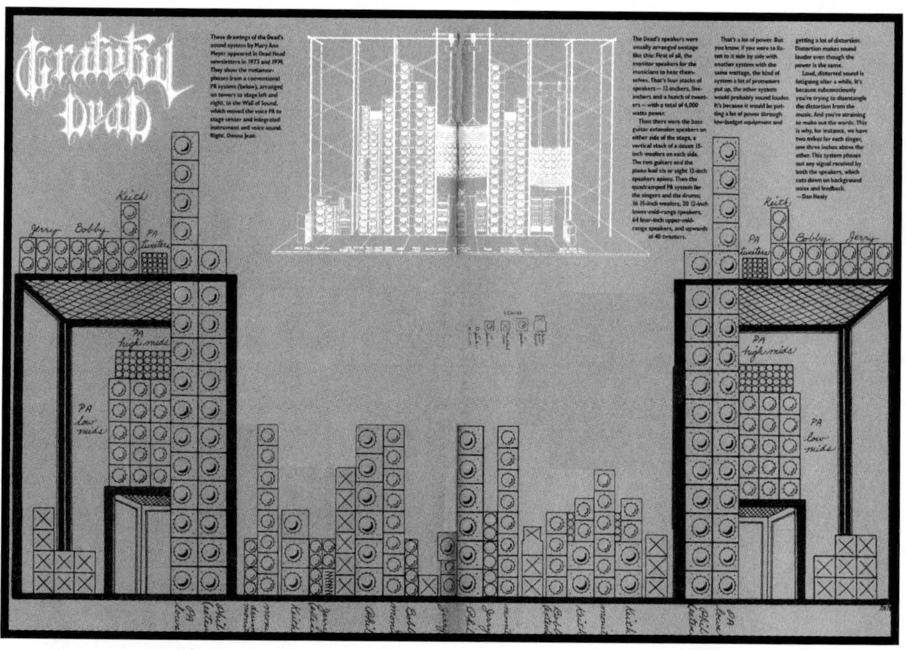

These drawings of the Dead's sound system by Mary Ann Meyer appeared in Dead Head newsletters in 1973 and 1974. They show the metamorphosis from a conventional PA system (below), arranged on towers to stage left and right, to the Wall of Sound, which moved the voice PA to stage center and integrated instrument and voice sound. Right, Donna Jean.

The Dead's speakers were usually arranged onstage like this: First of all, the monitor speakers for the musicians to hear themselves. That's four stacks of speakers—12-inchers, five-inchers and a bunch of tweeters—with a total of 4,000 watts power.

Then there were the bass guitar extension speakers on either side of the stage, a vertical stack of a dozen 15-inch woofers on each side. The two guitars and the piano had six or eight 12-inch speakers apiece. Then the quadramped PA system for the singers and the drums: 16 15-inch woofers, 20 12-inch lower-mid-range speakers, 64 four-inch upper-mid-range speakers, and upwards of 40 tweeters.

That's a lot of power. But you know, if you were to listen to it side by side with another system with the same wattage, the kind of system a lot of promoters put up, the other system would probably sound louder. It's because it would be putting a lot of power through low-budget equipment and getting a lot of distortion. Distortion makes sound louder even though the power is the same.

Loud, distorted sound is fatiguing after a while. It's because subconsciously you're trying to disentangle the distortion from the music. And you're straining to make out the words. This is why, for instance, we have two mikes for each singer, one three inches above the other. This system phases out any signal received by both the speakers, which cuts down on background noise and feedback.

—Dan Healy

I cannot tell you how much I love to play for people ... Sometimes when I sit down to practice and there is no one else in the room, I have to stifle my impulse to ring for the elevator man and offer him money to come in and hear me.

—Arthur Rubinstein

When I'm singing, I'm inside of it.... I feel, oh, like I feel when you're first in love, when you're first touching someone—chills, things slipping all over me ... A lot of times when I get off, I want to make love.

—Janis Joplin

When I play, I make love—it is the same thing.

—Arthur Rubinstein

When we get onstage, we really want to be transformed from ordinary players to extraordinary ones, like forces of a larger consciousness. So maybe it's that seat-of-the-pants shamanism that keeps the audience coming back and that keeps it fascinating for us too.

—Jerry Garcia

When I'm onstage, I feel this incredible, almost spiritual experience. Those great rock 'n' roll experiences are getting harder and harder to come by, because they have to transcend a lot of drug-induced stupor. But when they occur, they are sacred.

—Pete Townshend

Sometimes my songs feel like drugs, they feel like injections. Depending on the song, sometimes they're like adrenalin, sometimes they make my bones shake, sometimes they're like a sedative. It's like hypos shooting different colours into my bloodstream. That's exactly what it feels like. And if my life experience hasn't given me the right chemicals, I can't sing those songs. I don't know how to bring it out of my own biochemistry.

—Kristin Hersh

It was easier to identify with the people in the Airplane than the Grateful Dead or Janis, because Janis was *so* powerful and *so* different, all the emotions right out there. The Grateful Dead looked like they were almost dead. They were just twenty years old, you know. But they were a *bizarre*-looking group of people. The people in the Airplane were like two-years-of-college white boys singing folk music. They were just more accessible on a pop-y kind of level.

—Grace Slick

The sign of a great talent to me? No one goes out to buy a *thing*. They sit and watch or stand and dance.

—Bill Graham

Musical instruments are alchemists' tools to change human energy from breath, from muscle, into sound. They are often the most elaborate and expensive tools found in many cultures—they are sculptures as well as voices. And playing a musical instrument is a physical as well as a mental activity. An instrument becomes an extension of the player's own body, and vibrating it is an intimate form of sensual play. The special power of a musical instrument comes from its construction. From the bodies of sacrificed animals or plants come drum membranes, gut strings, animal or human bone flutes, trumpets, slit-drums, and wooden bodies of string instruments. Thus, these sacred instruments are magical tools, and must be used with respect and awareness of their once-living spirit.

A musician goes to a smith to have a lute built for himself. After the instrument has been completed, the musician attempts to play it and declares that the lute has a bad sound. The smith answers: "This is a wooden thing. As long as it has no heart and experience, it cannot sing. It is you who must give it a heart and experience. The wood must go into battle on your back. The wood must echo with the sword blow. The wood must soak up the dripping blood: blood of your blood, breath of your breath. Its pain must become your pain and its fame your fame."

—Sudanese tale
(told by Marius Schneider)

It took me twenty years of study and practice to work up to what I wanted to play in this performance. How can she expect to listen five minutes and understand it.

—Miles Davis
(When a lady in the audience complained that she didn't understand what Miles Davis was playing.)

I'm not very good technically, but I can make it fuckin' howl and move.

—John Lennon

My music is best understood
by children and animals.

—Igor Stravinsky

I never practice, I always play.

—Wanda Landowska

If I don't practice for one day, I know it;
if I don't practice for two days,
the critics know it;
if I don't practice for three days,
the audience knows it.

—Ignacy Paderewski

Play always as if a master were listening.

—Robert Schumann

You know, I'm starting to feel pretty good. I know I've written some classic songs that someday are going to be elevator music, and that makes me feel pretty good.

—Christopher Cross

It is better to make a piece of music than to perform one, better to perform one than to listen to one, better to listen to one than to misuse it as a means of distraction, entertainment, or acquisition of "culture."

—John Cage

I read a story about some old opera singer once, and when a guy asked her to marry him, she took him backstage after she had sung a real triumph, with all the people calling for her, and asked, "Do you think you could give me that?" That story hit me right, man. I know no guy who ever made me feel as good as an audience.

—Janis Joplin

I am not handsome,
but when women hear me play,
they come crawling to my feet.

—Niccolò Paganini

Playing guitar is a sexual thing.
It comes from the crotch,
it comes from the heart,
and it comes from the head—
you don't need to have muscles to play it.

—Lita Ford

When you listen to what I'm playing,
you got to see in your mind
all them gals out there
swinging their butts
and getting the mens excited.
Otherwise you ain't got this music
rightly understood.
I could sit there and throw
my hands down
and make them gals do anything.
I told them when to shake it
and when to hold it back.
That's what this music is for.

—Robert "Fud" Shaw

When I'm playing, I'm in the now,
and I experience how I'm feeling
right there onstage,
and sometimes I'm able to get into a state
of 100% bliss.
It's a really joyous, serene place.

—Bill Kreutzmann

Music washes away from the soul
the dust of everyday life.

—Berthold Auerbach

The hardest part of playing is starting, getting up on stage and relaxing in the moment. Before you can share your music with others, you must reach for it inside yourself, in solitude. It is a form of meditation that sometimes takes many hours and sometimes comes in a flash.

The transition from this solitary state to the arena of public performance is critical and takes practice. Access All Areas is not granted freely. This is the point of no return, of great stress or great joy

I'd like to think that when I sing a song, I can let you know all about the heartbreak, struggle, lies and kicks in the ass I've gotten over the years for being black and everything else, without actually saying a word about it.

—Ray Charles

Don't think that sticking your boobs out and trying to look fuckable will help. Remember you're in a rock 'n' roll band. It's not "fuck me," it's "fuck you!"

—Chrissie Hynde
(advice to female rockers)

On stage, I make love
to 25,000 different people,
then go home alone.

—Janis Joplin

Romanticism, and sorrow, and greed—they can all be put into music. I can definitely recognize greed. I know when a man is playing for money.

—Coleman Hawkins

When it came to dollars, everyone got uptight. Probably the biggest bring down in my life was being in a pop group and finding out just how much it was like everything it was supposed to be against.

—Mama Cass Elliot

Real music is not for wealth,
not for honors
or even for the joys of the mind ...
but as a path for realization and salvation.

—Ali Akbar Khan

The adventure of composition is a mystery. As long as artists explore new territory, the compositional process will never be the same twice. The Muse has her ways, she hides from you, comes for you in the middle of the night, at midday, at dawn. You must be alert constantly. You must believe wholeheartedly in this divine power. We drink, take drugs, get straight, go to church, be good, be bad. We are always looking for inspiration. It is an elusive gift that can appear at any time, anywhere. Artists are in awe of it.

Think NOTHING
Wait until it is absolutely still
within you
When you have attained this
Begin to play
As soon as you start to think
STOP.
And try to retain
The state of NON-THINKING
Then continue playing.

—Karlheinz Stockhausen

The greatest respect an artist can pay to music is to give it life.

—Pablo Casals

There are two things John and I always do when we're going to sit down and write a song. First of all we sit down. Then we think about writing a song.

—Paul McCartney

The composer reveals the innermost being of the world and expresses the deepest wisdom in a language which his own reason does not understand; like a sleepwalker, who tells things of which he has no clear knowledge when he is awake.

—Arthur Schopenhauer

All I know is,
for every note,
there is another note that melts it.
I just hear a sound coming into my head
and hope to catch it with my hands.

—Erroll Garner

The notes I handle no better than
many pianists.
But the pauses between the notes—
ah, that is where the art resides!

—Artur Schnabel

The composer,
as in old China,
joins Heaven
and Earth
with threads
of sounds.

—Alan Hovhaness

When I listen to a Herbie Hancock piano solo, I listen with my hands. I can feel courses of melodies: my palms almost imperceptibly expand and contract, bursts of rapidity and repose make them tighten and relax; the fingers minutely follow the essential shapes and pacing of his improvisations.

—David Sudnow

Composing is like driving down a foggy road toward a house. Slowly you see more details of the house—the color of the slates and bricks, the shape of the windows. The notes are the bricks and mortar of the house.

—Sir Benjamin Britten

I believe it's no good to talk about your songs; it's wrong. You should leave your songs alone and let them say what they say; let people take what they want from them.

—Paul Simon

Not everybody can appreciate poetry or classical music, and they don't like words that say one thing and mean another thing. Country music is real. Country music tells the story the way things are. People fall in love and then one of 'em starts cheating around, or both of 'em sometimes. And usually there's somebody who gets hurt. Our country songs are nothing but the truth. That's why they're so popular.

—Loretta Lynn

There's this great line in a Chrissie Hynde song where she says, "When I first heard a song flying to the sun, I wanted to be one." You know, it's not that you want to sing the song, it's that you want to be one.

—Joan Osborne

To sing is to love and affirm,
to fly and to soar,
to coast into the hearts of the people
who listen,
to tell them that life is to live,
that love is there,
that nothing is a promise,
but that beauty exists,
and must be hunted for and found.

—Joan Baez

I love recording because if something lovely does happen, there is a sense of permanence, and if it doesn't happen, one has a second chance to achieve an ideal.

—Glenn Gould

We look for new sonorities,
new intervals,
new forms.
Where it will lead, I don't know.
I don't want to know.
It would be like knowing the date of my death.

—Pierre Boulez

Lovers have come and gone, but only my mistress stays. She is beautiful and gentle. She is a swinger. She has grace. To hear her speak, you can't believe your ears. She is ten thousand years old. She is as modern as tomorrow, a brand new woman every day. Music is my mistress, and she plays second fiddle to no one.

—Duke Ellington

When a songwriter dies, the minute you read the list of songs he wrote, you start to identify with him—"Oh, my God, he wrote that. I remember the first time I heard that song, I was at a dance with a girl."

—Abel Green

The public doesn't want new music; the main thing that it demands of a composer is that he be dead.

—Arthur Honegger

People compose for many reasons:
to become immortal;
because the pianoforte happens to be open;
to become a millionaire;
because of the praise of friends;
because they have looked into
a pair of beautiful eyes;
or for no reason whatsoever.

—Robert Schumann

With a perfect orchestra you can do what you like ... You can draw a sort of immense emotional throb out of the air merely by curving your hand.
You can get brilliant waves of sound merely by a twist of the wrist.
You can make sudden and absolute silence by a gesture.
It is the most wonderful of all sensations that any man can conceive.
It really oughtn't to be allowed.

—Eugene Goossens

The hardest thing in the world is to start an orchestra, and the next hardest, to stop it.

—Hans Richter

Music produces a kind of pleasure
that human nature cannot do without.

—Confucius

Music is the shorthand of emotion.
Emotions which let themselves be described in
words with such difficulty
are directly conveyed to man in music,
and in that is its power and significance.

—Leo Tolstoy

When I hear music, I fear no danger.
I am invulnerable.
I see no foe.
I am related to the earliest times,
and to the latest.

—Henry David Thoreau

A young composer once came to Mozart for advice on how to develop creatively. "Begin writing simple things first," Mozart told him; "songs for example." "But you composed symphonies when you were only a child," the man exclaimed. "Ah," Mozart answered, "but I didn't go to anybody to find out how to become a composer!"

—David Ewen

If a composer could state in words
what being a composer means,
he would no longer need to be a composer.

—Ned Rorem

For the first time with my physical ears I heard a sound that had kept recurring in my dreams as a boy—a high whistling C sharp. It came to me as I worked in my Westside apartment where I could hear all the river sounds—the lonely foghorns, the shrill peremptory whistles—the whole wonderful river symphony that moved me more than anything ever had before.

—Edgard Varèse

It's not like music begins or ends. All kinds of sounds are working into each other. Sometimes I'll just stop on the street because there's a sequence of sirens going on; it's like a melody I'll never hear again.

—Jeff Buckley

The song now known as "The Greatest Story Ever Told" was originally called "The Pump Song." I was living on a ranch in Novato, which in the 1970s and early 1980s was the band's communal home and gathering place. I built my first studio in the barn. Eventually the Anaconda would adorn its walls, making it the birthplace of my books. People would come and go twenty-four hours a day. It was a moveable feast, a continual party.

The one constant presence at the ranch was the sound of an old water pump, whose shaft went down over a hundred feet. Because it supplied all the water for the ranch, this pump went on and off continuously day and night. Its special rhythm became the rhythm of the land, imprinted on my consciousness, an interesting, insistent groove that varied slightly with the amount of water flowing—

interesting enough for me to lock onto and to provide a dependable vehicle for trance. When I think of the ranch now, it's the rhythm of the pump that first comes to mind.

At that time I was exploring the nature of sounds and the sounds of nature, and I was working on my first solo album, Rolling Thunder, which was like a musical family portrait of the year 1971. It occurred to me that since the pump was the rhythmic centerpiece of my soundworld, and since it directly related to the nurturing of the land, a recording of it would be an excellent basis for a composition. I put one microphone deep in the well's shaft and a second near the wellhead. This was one of my first field recordings.

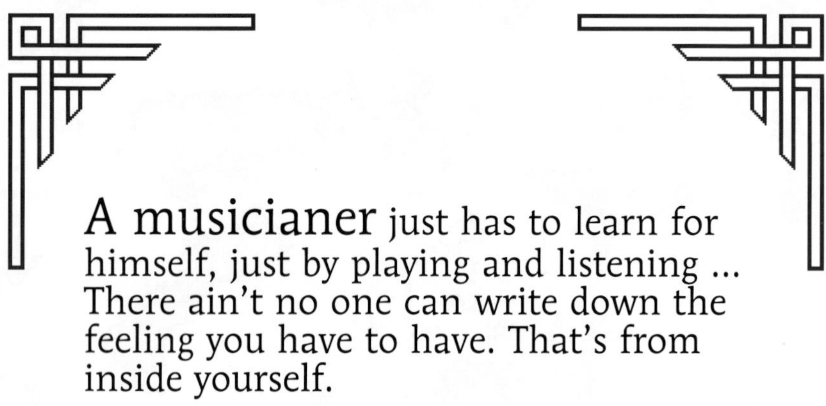

A musicianer just has to learn for himself, just by playing and listening ... There ain't no one can write down the feeling you have to have. That's from inside yourself.

—Sidney Bechet

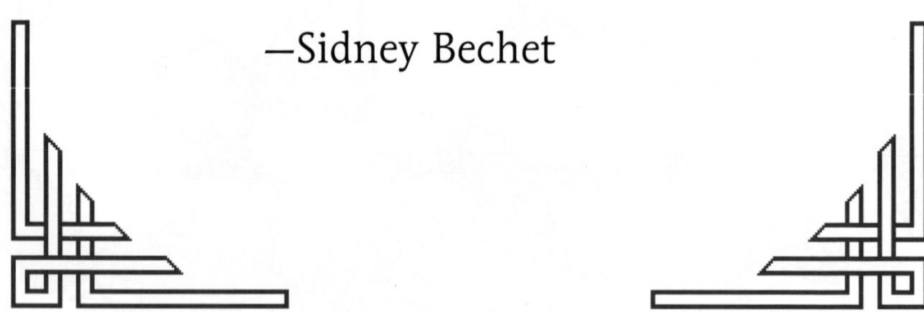

The first song I was listening to that my mother told me to turn the radio off was called "Natural, Natural Ditty." And if I only knew then what I know now, no wonder she wanted me to turn it off. I mean, that was the biggest boogie ever, man. That was it, you know. See, I didn't used to know what that was either. Because it's loud, that means it's rebellion. We like it loud, we like it, you know, the dissonance, when notes are bent and when the saxophones go crank, and the drums smash, instead of that polite little ch-ch-ch thing. All I know is it sounds good, and we really feel that way. It's like slamming the car door.

—Stu Cook

Improvisation is not the expression of accident but rather of the accumulated yearnings, dreams, and wisdom of our very soul.

—Yehudi Menuhin

The rest of the band will follow me down any dark alley. Sometimes there's a light at the end of the alley, and sometimes there's a black hole. The point is, you don't get an adventure in music unless you're willing to take chances.

—Jerry Garcia

My personal bond to shamanic culture is through the drum. The world of the shaman acknowledges the importance of rhythmic awareness. My Grateful Dead reality required a similar awareness, which enabled the band to create an environment in which a broad range of emotions could be freely expressed. When we were on, both the performers and the audience were aware of the transformational power of the experience. We had played through our personal repertoire of cliches and facile "licks" and had transcended the notes, entering another space entirely, discovering once again that the song is only a door or a passageway to one of many elemental worlds of music.

I have often asked myself how this happens. How does music serve as the catalyst for the alteration of consciousness?

Music exists in its own time-world, outside of clock time. The way I feel at a particular moment, what I bring to the stage, that is the pulse—that is all I truly have to relate to, not the clock. Music starts from this inner pulse—the heartbeat, the blood running, an awareness of how I feel.

When you are playing inside of the pulse, you can anticipate or relax, and you produce different emotions. When you speed up, you are anticipating. When you slow down, you are relaxed and secure, producing a different kind of groove, not just a steady metronomic beat. Billy Kreutzmann calls it massaging the beat. He says we massage it continuously, with constant small updates at incredible rates. Instead of playing off the clock, we are playing off the pulse of the ensemble's inner time, finding where it feels exactly perfect.

My transformation starts when the rhythm sets in motion a series of internal events, persuading my senses that a state of well-being and mutual trust exists among the musicians. In order to feel at one with this rhythm, I have to yield myself to it, not fight it. My inner reference point is my pulse. After initially addressing the drum, exciting it, and slowly balancing my relation to it, I become intellectually detached from my instrument, and my judgment rivets itself onto my emotions. I find myself in a gravity-less environment where both my arms and my drums alter perceptively in weight, size, and sometimes even in shape.

As I continually sense the response of the drum, it reveals its personality. The drum sound acts as a magnet. It demands my attention, drawing me inside by its power, presence and volume. My body rocks left to right, back and forth, reinforced by the hypnotic effect of the drums. My movements help to outline and maintain the larger units of time, and the inner divisions fit evenly into the larger rhythm of this cycle.

At the same time, the drum has undergone its own transformation. I am no longer aware of the instrument. It has joined forces with my emotions, making me feel as if it plays itself. The constant feedback I receive as I monitor the stick striking then recoiling from the head dictates the proper tempo and dynamic of what I will play. The rhythm depends on the tension and the tone of the drumhead. In this way the drum lives and has a unique voice of its own. I have seen my drumheads turn into their untanned furry state, the drum eventually becoming an extension of my hand, my entire body.

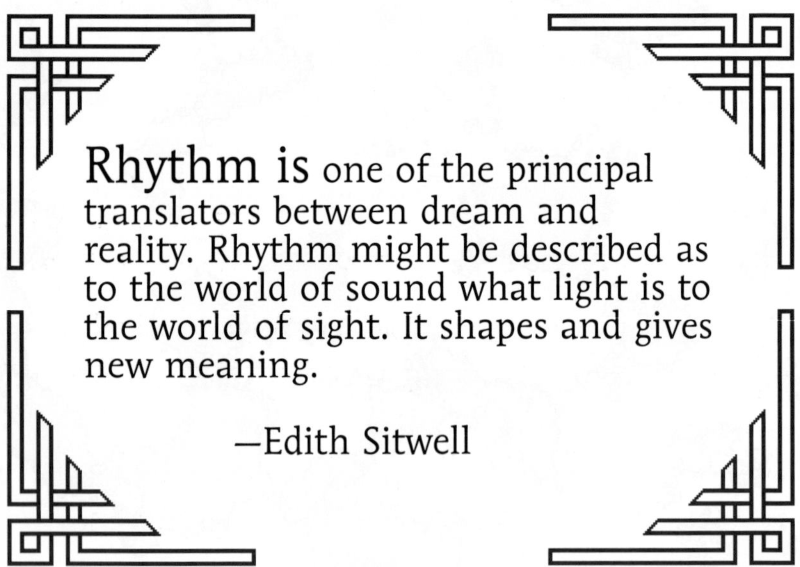

Rhythm is one of the principal translators between dream and reality. Rhythm might be described as to the world of sound what light is to the world of sight. It shapes and gives new meaning.

—Edith Sitwell

Chapter Two

Music and Society

The Global Tuning Fork

Music is color-blind. It doesn't know political or geographical boundaries, rich from poor, man from woman, weak from powerful, young from old. The creation of music requires harmonious cooperation, a unity of effort from everyone involved. To bring this energy together in the individual and the group–this is music as part of a global tuning fork.

Music can be used in this way, to bring balance to the world. Modern society, though more and more conscious of limited and polluted natural resources, is less aware of the sonic environment, the soundscape of the world. We have violated the integrity of the natural soundscape with noise pollution of all kinds, and we ignore the sonic element in the design of our private and public spaces. As a result the world is out of tune. As many have written, music is a natural way to resolve this imbalance.

John Blacking once told me that although music is a force that helped develop civilization, it is not solely a human invention. The use of music-like sounds for communication, mating rituals, warning, and definition of territory are found in many pre-human species. The human brain was formed as pre-humans used sound to express social and personal needs, thus creating the seeds of civilized society as we know it.

We pray with it,
Dance to it,
Sing and have fun with it,
We pass the day,
Drive the car,
Wash the windows,
Sip some wine.
We eat our meals,
Wash our clothes and
bury our dead with it.

The ability of music to open doors and make connections among people from different cultures is both quite common and at the same time extraordinarily powerful—another testimony to its magic and to its essential role in the tuning of the world.

On a 1998 trip to Bali to record some of the incredible music of that magical place, I asked Ketut Gede Asnawa, one of the senior Balinese scholars of music, to show me what he considered the finest recorded examples of their musical traditions. One of the CDs that he gave me was *Music for the Gods*, a collection of rare and formerly unpublished gamelan music from before the Second World War that I had produced for the Library of Congress the previous year. These recordings had been unknown in Bali, and they represented a musical period in their culture otherwise unavailable to them. Their discovery of this music was like the homecoming of a long-lost family member, very much like the welcome return of a prisoner of war, long thought to be dead.

I was, of course, proud and excited to think that the Balinese viewed this recording as a cultural treasure. When I showed them that I was the producer of this album, their natural courteous and welcoming manner changed dramatically. I was no longer just a respected musical tourist. I was now considered one of the family. As the word of my involvement with that project spread, the buzz of excitement among the musicians was palpable, and they went to great lengths to prepare for the recording sessions ahead. The energy in those sessions was electrifying.

There are two aspects of life:
the first is that
man is tuned by his surroundings,
and the second is that
man can tune himself
in spite of his surroundings.

—Inayat Khan

How we act,
how the vibrations of our music and speech
and actions reverberate in our environments,
obviously come back to us in many ways.
Tibetans and Indians call that karma.

—David Hykes

The cosmic system is working by
the law of music, the law of harmony;
and whenever that harmony in the
cosmic system is lacking in any way,
then in proportion disaster comes to
the world.

—Inayat Khan

The earth forms the body of an instrument, across which strings are stretched and are tuned by a divine hand. We must try once again to find the secret of that tuning …

—R. Murray Schafer

For there is a music where ever there is a harmony, order, or proportion: and thus far we may maintain the music of the Spheres; for those well-ordered motions, and regular paces, though they give no sound unto the ear, yet to the understanding they strike a note most full of harmony.

—Sir Thomas Browne

Musical hearing is among the highest achievements of which humans are capable, and it takes place simultaneously on various levels of the individual as a whole.
It is a psychic process,
since man is a being with a soul.
It is a social process,
since every man is also a fellow creature.
And it is a historical process,
since every man lives in a historical world.

—Helmut Reinold

He who lets his breath,
hence his life force,
flow consentingly as a willing sound sacrifice
from the depths of his body,
sings his life;
for singing means to affirm life,
to free oneself,
and thereby to bring happiness
and prosperity to oneself,
and consequently to one's fellow men.

—Marius Schneider

I did not discover music; music discovered me. During the dark years in Germany, as a child, I played Mozart on the piano and allowed the music to tune me. Music nourished and protected me ... Now, eighty years old, I find that music is still interconnecting me with the flow of cosmic energy that is infinite and far beyond all things material. We all are in the dance!

—Ruth-Inge Heinze

There will come a time when a diseased condition of the soul life will not be described as it is by psychologists, but it will be spoken of in musical terms, as one would speak, for instance, of a piano that was out of tune.

—Rudolph Steiner

Today we hear so much musical sound all the time, in trains, in airplanes, in restaurants, that we are becoming deadened to it.
Our sensitivity to music is in danger of being lost,
just as we are becoming insensitive
to the stupid brutality
we see so much on television
or in motion pictures.
Still, we are able to turn off television,
or walk out of a bad motion picture
or a poor concert.
You can't walk out of an airplane.

—Leopold Stokowski

We cannot close our ears; we have no ear lids.

—R. Murray Schafer

... If you're not playing beautiful music that takes people to another plane, to a delicious place that they can't ordinarily go in their own lives every day and show them beauty–what do I want to hear ugly sounds for? We hear all kinds of ugly sounds in the street. Why do I have to hear that coming from someone on the stage? I want delicious sounds, and beautiful horns and beautiful music put together so it'll take me away on a dream. *Dreams.* That's what it's all about–dreams. Without that there's nothing.

—Ruby Braff

Man has always tried to destroy his enemies with terrible noises.
We shall encounter deliberate attempts to reproduce the apocalyptic noise throughout the history of warfare,
from the clashing of shields and the beating of drums in ancient times
right up to the Hiroshima and Nagasaki atom bombs....
In antiquity, life was nothing but silence.
Today noise reigns supreme
over human sensibility ... in the pounding atmosphere of great cities
as well as in the formerly silent countryside.

—Luigi Russolo

Wherein lies the power of songs? Maybe it derives from the sheer strangeness of there being singing in the world.... That we should have discovered the magical intervals and distances that yield the poor cluster of notes, all within the span of a human hand, from which we can build our cathedrals of sound, is as alchemical a mystery as mathematics, or wine, or love.... Song shows a world that is worthy of our yearning, it shows us our selves as they might be, if we were worthy of the world.

Five mysteries hold the keys to the unseen: the act of love, and the birth of a baby, and the contemplation of great art, and being in the presence of death or disaster, and hearing the human voice lifted in song. These are the occasions when the bolts of the universe fly open and we are given a glimpse of what is hidden.... Glory bursts upon us in such hours: the dark glory of earthquakes, the slippery wonder of new life, the radiance of ... singing.

—Salman Rushdie

Music is the answer to the mystery of life.
The most profound of all the arts,
it expresses the deepest thoughts of life.

—Arthur Schopenhauer

Music does something to a person,
something not done by anything else;
nothing can be substituted for it....
We do not consider music to have
a single main function
except for being music,
but we feel we cannot live without it.

—Bruno Nettl

Music appeals to a part of our basic genetic code. World beat is based on local musics, a blend of the rhythms of ancient and modern, old world and new. What we call "world music" really is the world's music. It's a reflection of our dreams, our lives, and it represents every fiber of our being. It's an aural soundscape, a language of the deepest emotions; it's what we sound like as a people.

Grateful Dead became a melting pot of these many strains of the world's music. We could be a jug band, a raga band, a blues band, a marching band, a swing band, a gypsy band, or a ritual band. We were not stuck too deeply in any specific tradition but felt compelled to discover new roads and tease out new meanings from the musical experience of the moment.

With Planet Drum, I continue to explore the world's music.

You know, there's this place where a river runs into an ocean and the fresh water and the salt water all get mixed in together. And that's what America is all about, and that's what American music is about, and that's what rock 'n' roll is about. It actually wasn't invented by anybody, and it's not just black and white, either. It's Mexican and Appalachian and Gaelic and everything that's come floating down the river.

—T-Bone Burnett

I've developed this strong feeling about what's happening to so-called "primitive" and ethnic tribal peoples. I believe that the complexity of their music stands as a symbol of the richness of their societies, and I hope that people, upon listening to this music, might think that if these cultures can produce music this intricate and this intelligent, then they can't really be "primitive."

—Brian Eno

You got twelve notes. Those notes don't know the difference who's using them. Some of 'em are white, some of 'em are black.

—Quincy Jones

One Planet, One Music.

—MTV advertisement

All I can say is that when I was a boy, we always was singin' in the fields. Not real singing, you know, just hollerin'. But we made up our songs about things that was happening to us at the time, and I think that's where the blues started.

—Son House

You can't go by what the preacher say because he and the bluesman looking for the same thing—some money, some chicken, and a nice-looking woman.

—James "Son" Thomas

I love the blues,
they hurt so nice.

—Anonymous

Blues is a digging, picking,
pricking at the very depth
of your mental environment
and the feelings of your heart.
Blues is more than just blues.

—Thomas A. Dorsey

What we call low-down in blues doesn't
mean that it's dirty or bad or something like
that.
It gets down into the individual to set him on
fire,
dig him up
or dig her up way down there
'til they come out with an expression verbally.
If they're in the church,
they say, "Amen."
If they're in the blues,
they say, "Sing it now."

—Thomas A. Dorsey

The blues had a baby,
and they called it rock 'n' roll.

—Muddy Waters

Rock's noise has been necessary to break through the crust of self-consciousness accumulated over these last three thousand years. So that a place long asleep in us would wake. In the instant environment of rock, the literally deafening noise cancels out the rest of the culture.

—Michael Ventura

The Rolling Stones found the frequency, they sounded the chime, they dripped the tap on to the bucket, they cracked the mirror and busted the glass. "Satisfaction" can never be unwritten.

—Germaine Greer

The effect of rock 'n' roll on young people is to turn them into devil worshippers; to stimulate self-expression through sex; to provoke lawlessness, impair nervous stability, and destroy the sanctity of marriage.

—Rev. Albert Carter

I declare that the Beatles are mutants. Prototypes of evolutionary agents sent by God, endowed with a mysterious power to create a new human species—
a young race of laughing freemen.

—Timothy Leary

"Pop tune" does not mean
that your pop song
just came out last week.
Lots of new tunes are not popular with the people, and lots of new tunes will be sung and loved by all of us a thousand years from now.

—Woody Guthrie

I guess all songs is folk songs.
I never heard no horse sing 'em.

—Big Bill Broonzy

I never even heard
any song called a folk song.
After all, every song is a song by folks
and for the folks.
I don't recall ever writing any songs for cows,
chickens, fish, monkeys, nor wild animals
of any kind.

—Woody Guthrie

Jazz is people talking,
laughing,
crying,
building,
painting,
mathematicizing,
abstracting,
extracting,
giving to,
taking from,
making of.
In other words, living.

—Willis Conover

Hot can be cool
and cool can be hot,
and each can be both.
But hot or cool, man,
jazz is jazz.

—Louis Armstrong

There'll probably be new names for it.
There have been several names
since I can remember
back to the good ol' days
in New Orleans, Louisiana,
when Hot Music was called "ragtime music,"
"jazz music,"
"gut bucket music,"
"swing music,"
and now "hot music." So
you see instead of dying out,
it only gets new names.

—Louis Armstrong

Jazz is
the only music in which the same note
can be played
night after night
but differently each time.

—Ornette Coleman

Thus it came to pass
that jazz multiplied all over the face of the earth and the wriggling of bottoms was tremendous.

—Peter Clayton

Rock won't eliminate your problems.
But it will let you sort of dance all over them.

—Pete Townshend

The turning point
in the history of Western civilization
was reached with the invention
of the electric guitar.

—Leni Sinclair

Jam sessions,
jitterbugs and canni-
balistic rhythmic orgies
are wooing our youth
along the primrose
path to hell!

—The Most Rev.
Francis J. L. Beckman

Civilization is spread more by singing
than by anything else,
because whole big bunches can sing a particular song
where not every man can join in
on the same conversation.
A song ain't nothing
but a conversation fixed up
to where you can talk it over and over
without getting tired of it.

—Woody Guthrie

Music's matter is sound and
motion of body.

—Aristides Quintilianus

Sound is an event:
by its coming it breaks an original silence,
and it ends in a final silence.
Music is born,
develops,
and realizes itself within silence:
upon silence it traces out its moving arabesques,
which give a form to silence
and yet do not abolish it.

—Gisèle Brelet

Music is nothing else
but wild sounds civilized into time and tune.

—Thomas Fuller

In the beginning
was silence,
womb of all words which all words seek,
mother of these:
breath of my life ...
Perhaps sound is only an insanity of silence,
a mad gibber of empty space
grown fearful of listening to itself
and hearing nothing.

—Steven Millhauser

Singing together unites those who disagree, makes friends of those at odds, brings together those who are out of charity with one another. Who could retain a grievance against the man with whom he had joined in singing before God?

—St. Ambrose

Music is no different than opium.
Music affects the human mind
in a way that makes people think of nothing
but music and sensual matters ...
Music is a treason to the country,
a treason to our youth,
and we should cut out all this music
and replace it with something instructive.

—Ayatollah Khomeini

The phenomenon of music is given to us with the sole purpose of establishing an order in things, particularly the co-ordination between man and time.

—Igor Stravinsky

The voice is not only indicative
of man's character,
but it is the expression of his spirit.
Other sounds can be louder than the voice,
but no sound can be more living.

—Inayat Khan

I can tell you much more
about what a man is really thinking
by listening to him play
than by hearing him talk.
You can't hide anything in that horn.

—Jo Jones

A drum circle is not a professional ensemble, nor is it really about music, but rather a group of friends casually having a rhythm party.

The drum circle is about rhythm and noise. And what a noise! The acoustical mass of many similar instruments playing together and agreeing on a common groove, with no soloists, leads to auditory driving without the artificial assistance of a PA system. Sensory overload gives birth to ritual, rapture, and trance.

Since this is a huge jam session, the unexpected always happens. The ultimate goal is not precise rhythmic articulation or perfection of patterned structure, but the ability to entrain and reach the state of a group mind. Since this is a new tradition we make the rules as we go ... Rules can be broken, because there is an anti-authoritarian essence to the circle. It is built to be a free space just this side of chaos. It is built on cooperation in the groove, but with little reference to any classic styles. So this is a work in constant progress, a phenomenon of the new rhythm culture emerging here in the West.

On many occasions performing with Grateful Dead or Planet Drum, I've noticed that the band achieves such a level of synchrony that the audience just has to reinforce the rhythm by clapping in unison. No one starts it, no one directs it. It's a social response to the power of the groove.

Where I come from we say that rhythm
is the soul of life,
because the whole universe revolves
around rhythm,
and when we get out of rhythm,
that's when we get into trouble.

—Babatunde Olatunji

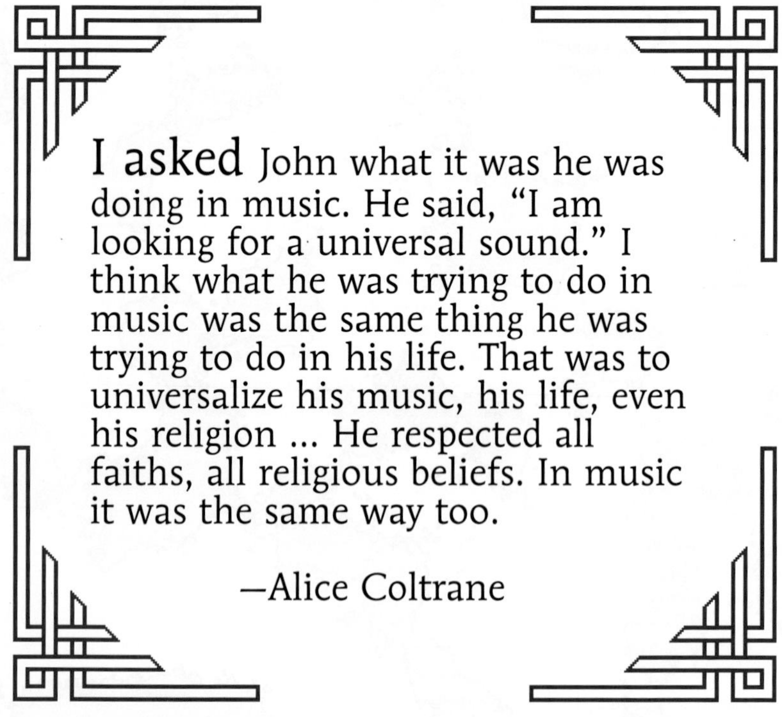

I asked John what it was he was doing in music. He said, "I am looking for a universal sound." I think what he was trying to do in music was the same thing he was trying to do in his life. That was to universalize his music, his life, even his religion ... He respected all faiths, all religious beliefs. In music it was the same way too.

—Alice Coltrane

It's a rhythmic universe we live in; everything alive spins and oscillates in rhythm. The rhythm laws of order and chaos seem to be the standard building blocks of nature. Rhythm is also the glue that ties together random or external phenomena outside our direct control. The sea, the heavens, the wind, and the stars dance their own rhythmic dance until eternity.

Let's walk together through a great modern capital, with the ear more attentive than the eye and we will vary the pleasures of our sensibilities by distinguishing among the gurgling of water, air and gas inside metallic pipes, the rumbling and rattlings of engines beating with obvious animal spirits, the rising and falling of pistons, the stridency of mechanical saws, the loud jumping of trolleys on their rails, the snapping of whips, the whipping of flags. We will have fun imagining our orchestration of department stores' sliding doors, the hubbub of crowds, the different roars of railroad stations, iron foundries, textile mills, printing houses, power plants and subways.

—Luigi Russolo

No human culture has ever existed without music.

Music is a necessity.
It is not just for survival or
for entertainment.

Music makes us human.

There is certainly no action among men that is carried out without music. Sacred hymns and offerings are adorned with music, specific feasts and the festal assemblies of cities exult in it, wars and marches are both aroused and composed through music. It makes sailing and rowing and the most difficult of the handicrafts not burdensome by providing an encouragement for the work.

—Aristides Quintilianus

Songs are a map of people's experiences, and that's the way you connect to them.

—Steven Feld

I ask you, Mister President,
please let everybody everywhere sing all night long. Love songs, work songs, new hope songs.
This will cure every soul in our jail, asylum,
and sick in our hospital, too.
Try it and see.
I know. I am a prophet singer.

—Woody Guthrie

If music can serve to further civilization,
then it has performed its ultimate goal.

—Bob Weir

The music of a well-ordered age
is calm and cheerful,
and so is its government.
The music of a restive age is excited and fierce,
and its government is perverted.

—Chinese classic

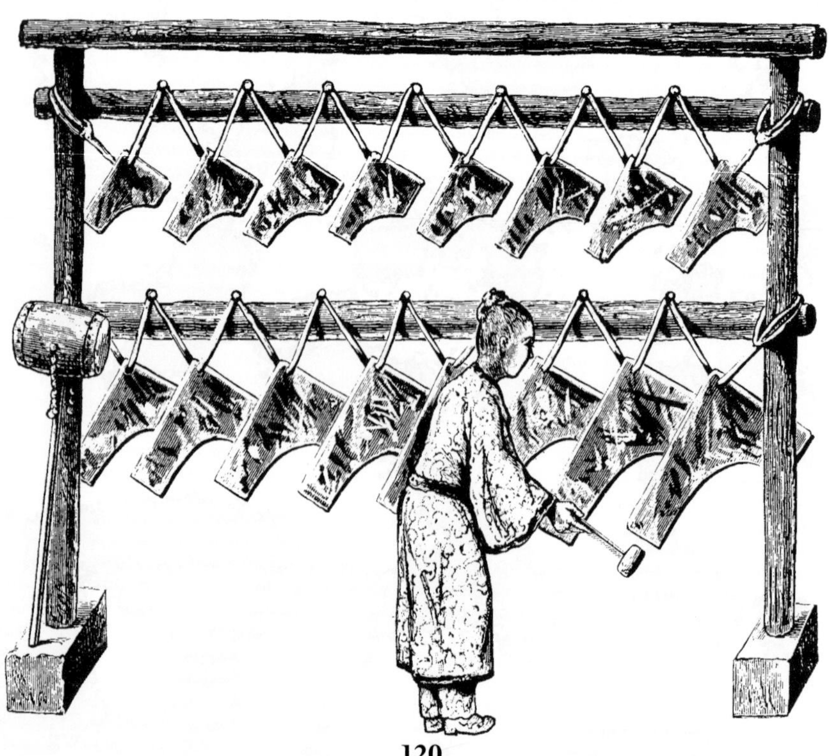

Of the many domains of culture,
music would perhaps seem to be
one the least necessary;
yet we know of no culture that does not have it.

—Bruno Nettl

The man who disparages music as a luxury
and nonessential is doing the nation an injury.
Music now, more than ever before,
is a national need.

—Woodrow Wilson

There is a difference between
music that is occasional
and music that enhances human
consciousness,
music that is simply for having
and music that is for being.

—John Blacking

If the king loves music,
there is little wrong in the land.

—Mencius

Music leads every change,
for it is first in order
and power before all learning.

—Aristides Quintilianus

My essential purpose in singing
is to help the listener understand reality.

—Pete Seeger

The superior man tries to promote music
as a means to the perfection
of human culture.
When such music prevails,
and people's minds are led towards the right
ideals and aspirations,
we may see the appearance of a great nation.

—Confucius

The closest Western civilization has come to unity since the Congress of Vienna in 1815 was the week that the *Sgt. Pepper* album was released.

—Langdon Winner

All the wars which we see in the world, only occur because of the neglect to learn music.... Were all men to learn music, would not this be the means of agreeing together, and of seeing universal peace reign throughout the world?

—Molière

The best way to get to knowing any bunch of people is to go and listen to their music.

—Woody Guthrie

My stuff is definitely up for discussion. When you're listening to an Ice-T album you're listening to me in the middle of a park yelling out my attitudes, my ideas. You can agree or disagree. But you should never think everything I'm thinking 'cause then only one of us is thinking.

—Ice-T

People who make music together
cannot be enemies,
at least not while the music lasts.

—Paul Hindemith

For me, music is this magic acoustic
element that makes perfectly rational people
who have come to realize the unalterable fact
that they are truly alone in the world
somehow feel for fleeting moments that
maybe they're not alone after all.

—Billy Joel

I have always loved music; anyone who has skill in this art gains a good temperament, fitted for all things. We must teach music in schools; a schoolmaster must have skill in music. Neither should we ordain young men as preachers unless they have been well exercised in music.

—Martin Luther

Teaching music is not my main purpose.
I want to make good citizens.
If a child hears fine music
from the day of his birth,
and learns to play it himself,
he develops sensitivity,
discipline and endurance.
He gets a beautiful heart.

—Shinichi Suzuki

The popular music scene today is unlike any scene I can think of in the history of all music. It's completely of, by and for the kids, and by kids I mean anyone from eight years old to twenty-five. They write the songs, sing them, own them, record them. They also buy the records, create the market, and they set the fashion in the music, in dress, in dance, in hair style, lingo, social attitudes.

—Leonard Bernstein

Music and love are inseparable. Certain music tugs on the heartstrings, makes us remember a loving moment, brings to mind a gentle time or a pretty face. Music is one of the best aphrodisiacs, a powerful stimulant to the senses or a nostalgic reminder of the fires of youth, rekindling the flame of love. It creates an atmosphere for intimacy and connection.

Which of the two powers, Love or Music, can elevate man to the sublimest heights? It is a great problem, and yet it seems to me that this is the answer: "Love can give no idea of music; but music can give an idea of Love." Why separate them? They are the two wings of the soul.

—Hector Berlioz

The hard task is to love,
and music is a skill that prepares man
for this most difficult task.

—John Blacking

Chapter Three

Music and Spirit

Secret Places of the Soul

Music is a special energy. It is of this world, but it also acts as a bridge to the spirit world. Music is our connection to the hidden world of the soul, the subconscious that lies beneath waking states. It becomes a universal language, a spirit language, with the power to change consciousness.

To reach the spirit world, the Siberian shaman rides on his drum, the rhythm a vehicle of transportation. We can use the same vehicle to explore our own inner spaces: riding the rhythm, learning to control it, and discovering new places both inside and outside of our being.

The ability to fine-tune this vehicle on the super-highway of the senses is the technology of trance. In some cultures trance involves allowing one's body to become a host for visiting spirits; in other cultures, one's spirit travels outside the body to the spirit world. Either way, we are exploring ecstasy, rapture, and altered states.

Once, when I was seriously ill with a fever from a bad flu, I still had to perform, and during the four-hour performance the symptoms of my illness gradually disappeared. The music not only provided a cure, but also left me feeling exhilarated. This is by no means a rare experience, it has happened to me numerous times. In fact, I can't remember ever feeling worse after a musical performance. For me, music has always been an effective physician, a means of tapping the secret places of the soul, bringing together and healing the mind and body.

Music training is a more potent instrument
than any other,
because rhythm and harmony
find their way into
the secret places of the soul.

—Plato

Music is a spiritual doorway....
Its power comes from the fact that it plugs
directly into the soul,
unlike a lot of visual art or textual information
that has to go through the more filtering
processes of the brain.

—Peter Gabriel

When the real music comes to me—"the music of the spheres, the music that surpasseth understanding"—that has nothing to do with me, 'cause I'm just the channel. The only joy for me is for it to be given to me, and to transcribe it like a medium.... Those moments are what I live for.

—John Lennon

What is wonderful about music is that it helps man to concentrate or meditate independently of thought; and therefore music seems to be the bridge over the gulf between form and the formless. If there is anything intelligent, effective, and at the same time formless,
it is music.

—Inayat Khan

Life depends upon the rhythmic working
of the whole mechanism of the body.
Breath manifests as voice, as word, as sound;
and the sound is continually audible,
the sound without
and the sound within ourselves.

—Inayat Khan

Music can name the unnamable
and communicate the unknowable.

—Leonard Bernstein

O Pythagoras,
if music thus transports us into the skies,
it is because music is harmony,
harmony perfection,
perfection our dream,
and our dream is heaven....
There is no need to be great
if we can only be in harmony
with the order of the universe.

—Henri Frédéric Amiel

Sound plays an important role in the voicing of the universal mythos that we all share as a people. It defines and speaks for and about the subconscious, where our dreams are born and live. Music gives the soul this inner self-expression, a voice. It gives the soul a sound, the sound of the Muse. This Muse is a force, an energy that urges us to create sound in a vibratory world.

Because the world vibrates, it is appropriate that we use sound waves to communicate our deepest feelings. These secret places of the soul are a hotbed of emotions. Poets write about them, artists paint them, we sound-shapers bring this hidden universe to life using instruments to create a feeling or make a rhythm as we strive to interpret our innermost thoughts. Thus the greatest calling for the artist is as the interpreter of dreams, the one who brings to the surface the emotions, shapes, and feelings of the soul.

Has any one ever observed
that music emancipates the spirit?
gives wings to thought?
and that the more one
becomes a musician
the more one is also a philosopher?

—Friedrich Nietzsche

Music is the electrical soil
in which the spirit
lives,
thinks,
and invents.

—Ludwig van Beethoven

Music is a strange thing. I would almost say it is a miracle. For it stands half way between thought and phenomenon, between spirit and matter, a sort of nebulous mediator ... we do not know what music is.

—Heinrich Heine

All tones are born from the heart of man.
Sentiment being stirred within
manifests without as sound.

—Dane Rudhyar

There is nothing better than music as a means for the upliftment of the soul.

—Inayat Khan

Most people don't have any idea what improvisation is ... It means the magical lifting of one's spirits to a state of trance ... It means experiencing oneself as another kind of living organism, much in the way of a plant, a tree—the growth, you see, that's what it is ... It's not to do with "energy." It has to do with religious forces.

—Cecil Taylor

The funny thing about enlightenment is that it's like you're searching for something—say your hat—and you're tearing the house apart and suddenly you look in a mirror and you see it sitting on top of your head. Music is where I've experienced that. I'm in a flow, I'm in the zone, there's a definite shift in my consciousness, without desire, without my ego, without me thinking, oh wow, I'm playing great. Just experiencing it as a flowing, living moment.

—Vernon Reid

A person does not hear sound
only through his ears;
he hears sound
through every pore of his body.

—Inayat Khan

The aim of better listening
is not to hear more,
but to hear more clearly,
especially the call toward consciousness.

—David Hykes

This is what I have to say
about Bach's life work:
listen, play, love, revere—
and keep your mouth shut.

—Albert Einstein

Everybody should have his personal
sounds—
sounds that will make him
exhilarated and alive
or quiet and calm ...
One of the greatest sounds of them all
is utter, complete silence.

—André Kostelanetz

The drummer is an inspirer, a leader, and a prophet. The blow of the drumstick translates itself not merely into sound, but into a spiritual reverberation. The excitement we feel when we hear the drumbeat tells us this is the skeleton key that opens the door into the realm of the spirit.

All one's life is a music,
if one touches the notes rightly,
and in time.

—John Ruskin

Music makes time audible.

—Suzanne Langer

Nowadays I think of the musician's job as that of a psychopomp, someone who conducts spirits or souls to the other world. In Greek mythology, Hermes, the messenger, was a psychopomp, as was Charon, the boatman who ferried the dead across the river Styx to the Underworld.

Grateful Dead was a ferryman, a conduit, a bridge to the spirit world, and the band provided a musical experience that offered safe passage to the other side. It was kind, dependable, and trusted for this task.

Over many years, the audience and the band developed a relationship built on trust, and a dependable transportation system was the bottom line of that relationship. Acoustic alchemy was necessary for the successful completion of the round trip.

A rock concert is in fact a rite
involving the evocation
and transmutation of energy.

—William Burroughs

Soul is not about black or white music.
Soul is a physical manifestation of higher consciousness.
It's going from the right lobe straight out to the world,
using the physical body as a springboard for an insight....
Soul is a howling at the moon—
and having the moon respond.

—Daryl Hall

You can't mess with people's heads,
that's for sure.
But that's what music's all about,
messing with people's heads.

—Jimi Hendrix

Because I am a storyteller, I live by words. Perhaps music is a purer art form. It may be that when we communicate with life on another planet, it will be through music, not through language or words.

—Madeleine L'Engle

The little creatures in the UFOs must have figured out sex by now, and our cars, but the dreaming, and the praying, and the singing ... How to explain music to them?

—John Updike

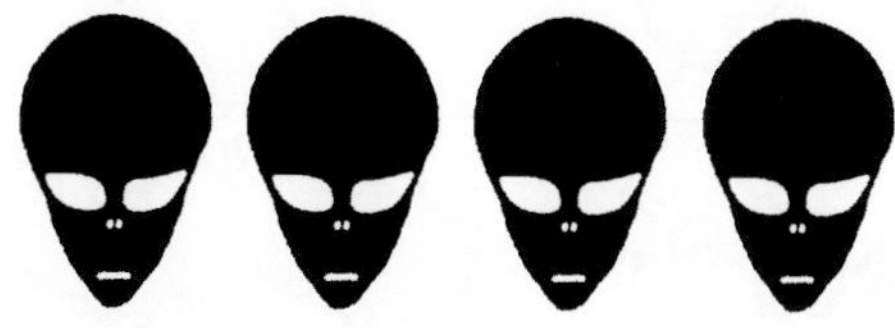

There is music in the air,
music all around us;
the world is full of it,
and you simply take as much as you require.

—Sir Edward Elgar

Some kinds of music dissipate in seconds.
Other kinds remain a lifetime,
stored in the limbs,
or maybe the brain,
or even the heart.

—Derrick de Kerckhove

Music has no other object than to brush aside the veil of everyday life, in order to bring us face to face with reality itself.

—Henri Bergson

The piece that seems long is the piece
that fails to suspend our consciousness
of real time.
The meaning of the music dies,
and we remember
that the hands of the clock are going round.

—Basil de Selincourt

One good thing about music,
when it hits,
you feel no pain.

—Bob Marley

Ouf!
Let me get out; I must have air.
It's incredible!
Marvelous!
It has so upset and bewildered me that when I wanted to put on my hat,
I couldn't find my head.

—Jean François Le Sueur
(writing about Beethoven's
Symphony No. 5)

We hide ourselves in our music to reveal ourselves.

—Jim Morrison

Music is our myth of the inner life.

—Suzanne Langer

Music is a kind of inarticulate,
unfathomable speech,
which leads us to the edge of the infinite,
and impels us for a moment to gaze into that!

—Thomas Carlyle

Music is the mediator
between intellectual and sensuous life ...
the one spiritual entrance into the higher world.

—Ludwig van Beethoven

Where speech fails,
then music begins.
It is the natural medium for the expression
too strong and deep to be expressed in words.

—Charles W. Landon

Music alone speaks at once to the imagination, the mind, the heart and the senses; and it is the reaction of the senses on the mind and heart, and vice versa, that produces the impressions felt by those who are gifted, but of which barbarians can know nothing.

—Hector Berlioz

Music is a language,
but a language of the intangible,
a kind of soul-language.

—Edward MacDowell

Music is not an escape from reality;
it is an adventure into the reality
of the world of the spirit.

—John Blacking

If the piece works poetically,
it takes me down a new path
from beginning to end.
Each piece should be like a journey—
and every journey is different.

—Earle Brown

The whole air seemed alive as if the tongues of those great cold, hard metal things had become flesh and joy. They burst into being screaming with delight and the city vibrated. Some wordless thing they said touched something so deep inside you that they made tears come.

—Emily Carr

Music sobs for you.
It laments,
it rejoices,
it explodes with vigor and life.

—Anaïs Nin

What happens to us when we wake from a deep sleep with a musical idea in our heads? What of the artist who sees an image for the first time in his or her dreams? The Muse rises and becomes a guiding light to these yet undiscovered areas of our subconscious, another reality where the images and sounds of the world of the soul reside. At night the conscious world declines in prominence, revealing another secret world, which contains the deepest thoughts brought to us sometimes in vivid detail, sometimes in a kaleidoscopic blur. This profusion of color and sound is what we call the Muse, the spirit watching over poets and artists, their source of inspiration.

Dreams emerge from the great
mystery mind.
They fill the head and heart
With images too rich to imagine.
These images,
Sounds,
Rhythms,
Reside in a place that is outside of our control.

They are not what we think we are,
Nor what we want to be.
They are what we really are.

The unconscious is the womb
of all musical creation;
all masterpieces are born there.

—Alan Walker

Music is the sort of dream architecture
which passes in filmy clouds
and disappears into nothingness.

—Percy A. Scholes

I'm just a voice speaking.
Anytime I'm singing about people,
and if the songs are dreamed,
it's like my voice is coming out of their dream.

—Bob Dylan

For is not music a language?
And of what is it the language?
Is it not the language of the dream world,
the world beyond thought?

—Robertson Davies

Chapter Four

Music and the Cosmos

The Sound of God

One of the shirts I sometimes wear announces boldly on its back that "God Is Sound." I believe that. To me God is a vibration, the original one, the sustaining one, the source of all cosmic and human energy.

We were born of noise, in chaos. The first sound in the universe was a noise. The big bang. The reverberations of that boom, still ongoing, were the source of cosmic rhythms, a dance of particles and atoms spinning out galaxies, stars, and planetary systems, finding its own groove, gradually bringing about order. That order is a harmony, incredibly involved and interdependent, like a heavenly clockworks. Awe-inspired ancients called it "the Music of the Spheres."

The process of human birth is no less a mystery, and it triggered my own musical response. The sound from the fetal monitor included among a host of gurglings and bodily noises, the emerging heartbeat of my unborn son Taro. It was the sound of a startling rhythmic event—the inner orchestra of emerging life, the rhythm world of the body at its most essential. It compelled me to entrain with it, to create new, complementary rhythms. As a father, the repetitive pulsing became symphonic in my mind; it drove me into the studio to create a new composition incorporating my son's living, developing, hopeful, amazing, unconscious, primordial music: *Music to Be Born By*.

The birth of new energy was essentially what Grateful Dead was all about. What I remember mostly from my early Dead experience was the spontaneous outpouring of group emotion. The music stimulated unchoreographed group movement, a new dance for a new day. And not only the music, but also the light show, taking over the visual field, overloading the senses, creating a whole-body experience, opening the gates of intuition. The options became unlimited.

I noticed for the first time a special connection between audience and musicians, in which the lines between them began to shimmer, blur, and soon disappear. What emerged was a group mind, creating its own performance, not heeding the traditional roles. The audience became a performer, and the band joined the audience.

The birth of the cosmos, a child, a new form of energy—all these are musical events in my mind. When I think of the "Sound of God," I think of a species-defining process that makes us human and nurtures us, the outpouring of the great ongoing symphony of life.

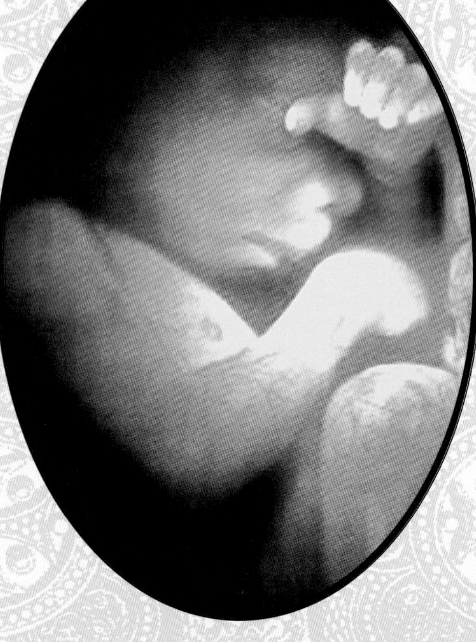

A sound precipitates air,
then fire,
then water
and earth—
and that's how the world
becomes.

—Joseph Campbell

First was the World as one great Cymbal made,
Where Jarring Windes to infant Nature plaid.
All Musick was a solitary sound,
To hollow Rocks and murm'ring Fountains bound.

Then Musick, the Mosaique of the Air,
Did of all these a solemn noise prepare
With which She gain'd the Empire of the Ear,
Including all between the Earth and Sphear.

—Andrew Marvell

Let me tell you,
music is a creation
of the almighty.
'Cause music was before everything else.
Before there was a wind
or the sound of a star moving through space;
that is all natural music—
it's the vibes of the music itself speaking,
different from the artist that's singing.
Music have plenty power.

—Ziggy Marley

Before God created man, he created the universe of souls. He then ordained that the seven planets and all the celestial spheres be set in motion. The souls then heard the divine harmony of creation. Then God created Adam and blew Adam's soul into his body. Adam's soul knew the divine harmony of the universe. Then God made Adam's heart to beat in rhythm with creation, and Adam sang aloud the praises of God and his creation.

—Sufi tale

God made a statue of clay in his own image,
and asked the soul to enter into it;
but the soul refused to be imprisoned,
for its nature is to fly about freely.
Then God asked the angels to play their music.
Moved to ecstasy,
the soul then entered the body.

—Hafiz

In the face of the power and beauty of music and its mysterious and magical nature, people throughout time have created myths to account for its origin. Since it was felt that "inventing" music was so clearly beyond the capabilities of ordinary people, cultural myths often attribute the origins of music to the gods.

Everything that throbs,
moves,
or stirs,
sunlit summer days,
nights when the wind howls,
the twinkling of stars,
the singing of birds,
the murmuring of trees,
blood moving in the veins in the silence
of the night—
everything that is, is music;
all that's needed is that it should be
heard.

—Romain Rolland

Whatever the gods do, they do by song. The song is the sacrifice.

—Shatapata Brahmana

When Zeus created the world he summoned the gods to show them his work. The gods came and admired the creation in silence. Since none of them said anything about this work, Zeus asked whether anything was still missing.

Then the gods answered:

"Your work is great and glorious, but the voice that would praise the great work is missing."

Thereupon Zeus created the Muse, for the existence of things is not complete as long as there is no voice to express it.

—Greek myth

God created the universe
in order to hear music,
and everything has a song of praise for God.

—Louis Ginsberg

The power of music is so great that
in legends of all nations
its invention is ascribed to the gods.

—Karl Marx

To some of us
the thought of God is like a sort of
quiet music played
in the background of the mind.

—William James

Music soothes us, stirs us up;
it puts noble feelings in us;
it melts us to tears, we know not how:
it is a language by itself,
just as perfect, in its way,
as speech, as words;
just as divine, just as blessed ...
Music has been called the speech of angels;
I will go further, and call it
the speech of God himself.

—Charles Kingsley

The listening experience consists of
hearing with a spiritual ear
the singing of all things in creation
praising the glory of God,
and in seizing and enjoying
the significance of this.

—Mircea Eliade

Music is one of the greatest gifts
that God has given us:
it is divine
and therefore Satan is the enemy.
For with its aid many dire temptations
are overcome; the devil does not stay
where music is.

—Martin Luther

Music is another planet.

—Alphonse Daudet

Music praises God.
Music is well or better able to praise him than the building of the church and all its decoration; it is the Church's greatest ornament.

—Igor Stravinsky

With celestial harmony,
music moves the earthly passions.

—Gioacchino Rossini

Every place we play is church.

—Phil Lesh

Music is often the preferred medium for communication with the gods. Speech gains magical potency when it rides on a melody or rhythm. Sung prayers are more powerful than spoken ones.

Every nation,
every human being that came across earth
had a song
and sang in some way to their God.

—Thomas A. Dorsey

There are many ways leading to God;
I have chosen that of music and dance.

—Rumi

To dance is to meditate
because the universe dances.
And, because the universe dances,
"He who does not dance
does not know what happens."

—Michael Ventura

Among the various things that are suitable for man's recreation and pleasure, music is the first and leads us to the belief that it is a gift of God set apart for this purpose.

—John Calvin

Music requires faith. You can't travel into the realm of the sacred unarmed. Music is staring at the burning bush.

—Elizabeth Cohen

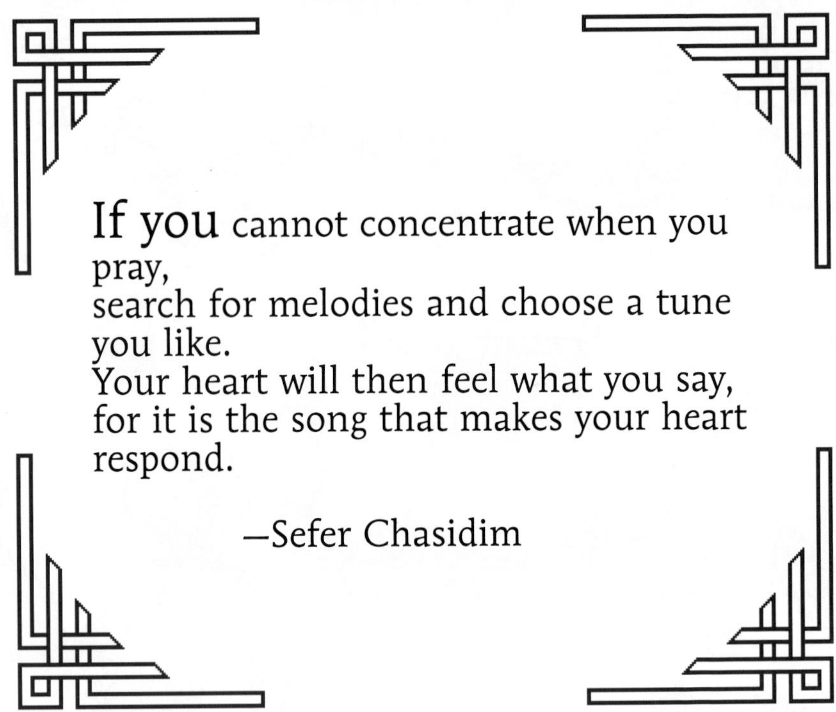

If you cannot concentrate when you pray,
search for melodies and choose a tune you like.
Your heart will then feel what you say,
for it is the song that makes your heart respond.

—Sefer Chasidim

Without music, life would be a mistake....
I would only believe in a God
who knew how to dance.

—Friedrich Nietzsche

In the ears of the believer, music becomes a new language, the language of God. It is a secret call whose intention is to make contact with yourself, to vibrate the mind and body, to form a union with the spirit world, and to send a message out to the unknown. We do not know the exact address, but we believe that Someone Is Listening. Music is the primary method of delivery—sometimes a group experience, sometimes solitary and private.

It was twenty-five years ago that, on a full moon night in October, high on the foothills of the Himalayas, there first broke upon my ears the holiest sound I have ever heard. The solo chords of the Gyuto monks have impounded Tibet's mystery into sound—a sound so awesome, so ethereal, that it verges on a vocal miracle.

—Huston Smith

All true and deeply felt music,
whether sacred or profane,
journeys to heights
where art and religion can always meet.

—Albert Schweitzer

For a musician, music is the best way to unite with God.

—Inayat Khan

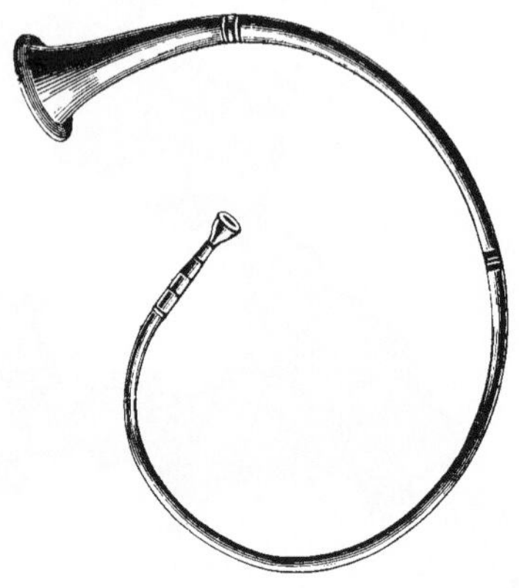

Sound is vibration, the pulsing of air. Organizing these vibrations brings us to music. The skilled and caring use of these orphan echoes, the very sounds that blew us into physical creation, brings us nearer to the edge of magic.

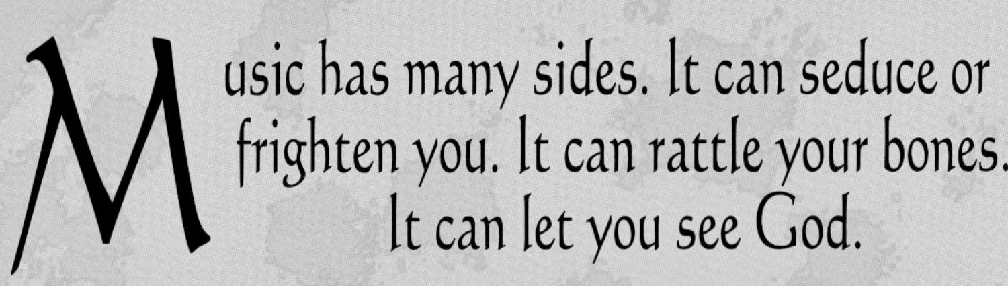

Music has many sides. It can seduce or frighten you. It can rattle your bones. It can let you see God.

When the concept of the rotating magnetic field was revealed to Tesla, he had seen in a flash the universe composed of a symphony of alternating currents with the harmonies played on a vast range of octaves. The 60-cycles-per-second AC was but a single note in a lower octave. In one of the higher octaves at a frequency of billions of cycles per second was visible light. To explore this whole range of alternating current and light waves, he sensed, would bring him closer to an understanding of the cosmic symphony.

—Margaret Cheney

Music is the harmonious
voice of creation,
an echo of the invisible world.
—Giuseppe Mazzini

The breath is your essence. It represents life, both physically and spiritually. The Word is carried on the breath. The Chinese knew it as qi, the life essence, the life force. The Hindu sages encapsulated the universal life force as Om, the sound of all that is, vibrating together, the sound of Gaia. The Shoshone believed that the breath is the sacred carrier of the message that embodies your essence in sound.

Music, being identical with heaven,
isn't a thing of momentary thrills....
It's a condition of eternity.

—Gustav Holst

Music is well said to be the speech of angels:
in fact, nothing among the utterances allowed
to man is felt to be so divine.
It brings us near to the infinite.

—Thomas Carlyle

Until I die there will be sounds.
And they will continue following my death.
One need not fear about the future of music.

—John Cage

All things shall perish from under the sky.
Music alone shall live—never shall it die.
There will always be music.

—Rita Marley

Music is ...
a labyrinth
with no beginning
and no end,
full of new paths to discover,
where mystery remains eternal.

—Pierre Boulez

Epilogue

The ancient world knew well the many powers of music, and used it in healing and ritual on a daily basis. In modern Western civilization, music has become a commodity, a product for mass consumption.

Today we acknowledge the need to bring the cycle around once again, and to rediscover the ancient wisdom of music as a healing force. In the modern world, however, it is not the priests or sages who will bring about this reconnection, but rather individuals on an unorchestrated, unchoreographed quest for self-knowledge, with science validating the ancient techniques and leading us to the next frontier. Experiments involving measurements of brain waves and the somatic response to music are in their infancy, but they will lead us to a better understanding of the healing capacity of music.

We don't fully comprehend the power of music and

probably never will. But this we know: music will have a crucial role in creating well-being by transcending politics, race, geography, and gender. Letting ourselves go, releasing daily pressures, and just plain having fun is not easy. With the world spinning faster and faster, play is ever more essential to maintaining balance and harmony.

To find ourselves, we need tools for self-exploration, and music is one of the most important. It enhances our lives and gives them meaning. It allows us to rediscover our lighter, softer side in an often hostile world. It gives us happiness and compassion, and it generates love. This is the bottom line of the musical experience—love. Love of self, family, neighbors, and friends. Music is a uniting force, capable of joining enemies in song and dance, enhancing the health of body and soul, and revealing that we are not so different after all.

All we need is a groove to move our feet, and songs to raise our spirits.

There was thunder in the floor, and I felt his presence with us, and I knew that music could always roll the stone from his tomb, and I knew, right then, no tomb could ever hold Elvis or his music. He would never die, and he would never leave us, and we could go on loving Elvis forever, and him living forever and his music living forever. He had passed through time, like water or steam through a sieve. His music fell on us like spring rain, and we were, all of us, ready to grow again.

—Kay Sloan and Constance Pierce

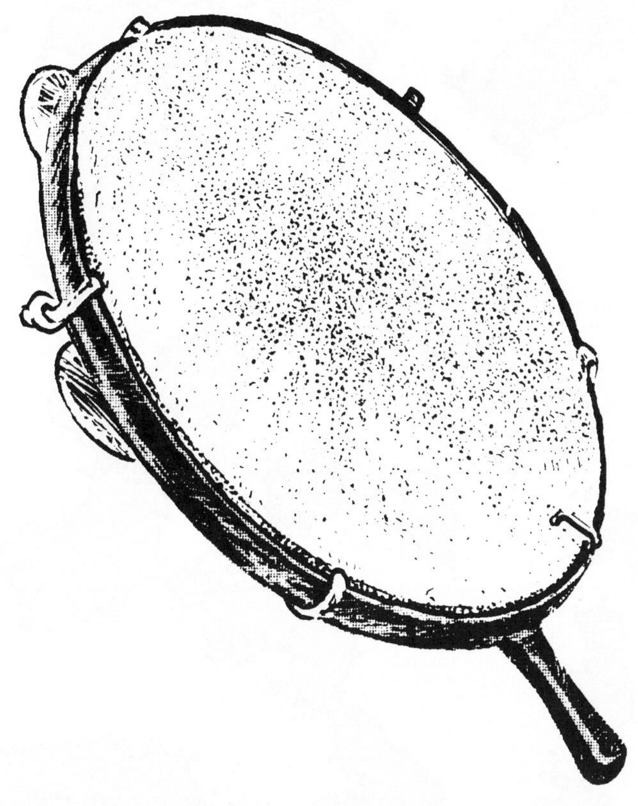

Glossary/Index

Driving down to Fiddler's Green to hear a tune or two
I thought I saw John Lennon there, looking kind of blue
I sat down beside him, said: "I thought you bought the store"
He said: "I heard that rumor, what can I do you for?"
"Have you written anything I might have never heard?"
He picked up his guitar and strummed a minor third
All I can recall of what he sang, for what it's worth:
"Long as songs of mine are sung I'm with you on this earth."

—Robert Hunter
(from "Down the Road")